FALSE MAPS FOR OTHER CREATURES

FALSE MAPS
FOR OTHER CREATURES

JAY MILLAR

A blewointment BOOK

NIGHTWOOD EDITIONS

ROBERTS CREEK, BC

2005

Nightwood Editions
R.R. #22, 3692 Beach Ave.
Roberts Creek, BC
Canada V0N 2W2

Edited for the house by Silas White
Typesetting by Carleton Wilson
Cover & inside drawings by Jesse Huisken

We gratefully acknowledge the support of the Canada Council for the Arts and the British Columbia Arts Council for our publishing program.

Printed and bound in Canada.

LIBRARY AND ARCHIVES CANADA CATALOGUING IN PUBLICATION

Millar, Jay, 1971-
False maps and other creatures / Jay Millar.

Poems.
ISBN 0-88971-203-4

I. Title.

PS8576.I3157F34 2005   C811'.54   C2005-901391-5

Contents

9   Space Gallery

Across Southwestern Ontario

13   The Pace of Creatures

14   One Afternoon

15   Passages

21   Author Photos

24   Facsimile

25   Fact's Mile

26   8th Concession, Tilbury, Ontario

28   Reception

30   Green

37   Three Specimen of Mushrooms:

40   Six Species of Insect:

Sum Lakes

49   Sum Lakes

50   Back Seat News

51   Shore Song

52   Call of the Wild

54   Gleyed

56   Canoe

57   Pine Trees

58   Hovercraft

59   Short Story

60   Variations on a Sentimental Poem

64   Nearby, Lakes

65   Fishing

66   Some Lakes

URBAN IN ENTITY

69   Day 232

71   Sonnets from the Protegé

80   Lakeshore

81   Let's Call These Poems St. Clair Avenue

89   Two Blocks

90   Last Poem

92   Some Literary History

94   Some Notes and Thanks

Space Gallery

What could one write but the small white
flowers in this petal's dreamed arrangement?
It is not a dream. It is a thing which flows,
                              how awe evolves

reason. Entire ecosystems have disappeared.
There exists a number of interesting studies
to demonstrate this subtle power
                              but you were asleep

on the other side of the room, beneath the
soft wild explosion, a portrait. That was my
idea: a sad old man draped in an array
                              of knowledge

extracted from another time, another place.
Someone died down the street. He was a
man, a father, a poet, somebody or other.
                              They sent an ambulance

but you would have preferred to receive
a small patch of land planted with grasses
to watch as they sprinkled your ashes
the field waving against the sky, saying
                              hello to the sun.

ACROSS SOUTHWESTERN ONTARIO

ACROSS SOUTHWESTERN ONTARIO

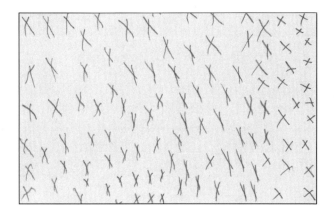

THE PACE OF CREATURES

These words follow more than
two hundred years of creatures who
rely on a city. It takes so long
to understand the beauty of such species
or such words. Each of us walks in turn
with no memory of where we began
though the range of our motion
will rise with the appearance of
consciousness and go do whatever, unaware
that language is present to tame us.

We shall continue at this pace
until the moment of our escape
for it has been ordained
that one after the other will fall free
or will be felled by gravity
and when the data has been compiled
all that shall remain untouched by the signal
will no longer require those particular
muscles that were too slow
to evolve beyond it in the first place.
And as the opportunity to respond
flies quietly toward the senseless, there
won't be anyone to say I told you so.

One Afternoon

Then suddenly the weather changed
a weak sun cast everything in
moisture as dissected brown or
green as abstract yellow

The ground expands a little wiser
waiting for a foot to arrive
the next logical impression
patches of rain in the distance

Weather patterns being weather
spaces for a mixture of spheres
the voices are not ours but
those which continue to speak

The thin nearby squawk of birds
a murder of crows calling
from across the cornfield
small lines of ink caught black

Marks against a strange sky
until the pause to peel
the bark from a silver birch
emerging from the woods

The rain or at least the idea of it
off in the distance beyond
what is defined as lines of green
or layers of an organism cultured

Between the edge of the woods
and the words of the edge's last leaf

PASSAGES

I

odd inscription –

the dead
old sheath of pickaxe
left for the fire

left unsettled
        burned

how could you know
the future's history?

        outside
snowflakes against the
stacked moon
sounds through the window
a long vowel filled with plots

fractures
half-remembered
and frozen

*

to think that the outstanding feature of their character
was their unfailing sympathy for the outcast and the underdog

*

is it evident
we make ourselves

how you speak

evidence

*

fossil

memory

crumble

as the last sequence
fire erases from the shale
exactly what it brings to the light

*

their puzzle remains
stillness stands in the
picture of a window

*

one must look through
time as landscape

instead of at the land
as an escape from how

over the years
things go awry

like leaves
after so much rain

*

      as one is
spoken on the wind
      spoken as birds
speak of the wind
in notes
dropping as they rise

green insists
within our seasons

what fades
brown white winter
in your bones

*

II

his head held back
with his eyes closed

paying attention in
that way he could

wood grain as motion
dead at Highway 2

view of the next hill
painted silver

in an eye
the perfect stillness

sky
broken

*

to say 'I look at it
differently now.'

a place where he lived
rode out of one day

and never came back
a place I wasn't

thinking about last week
as much as I am today

a place
I grew up

left and remember
from the odd angle

of the present
shades of grey

in the shadows of smallness
along a stretch of highway

happy on a bicycle
and all the memory I

choose to invent

III

who else
has gone

or else where
should some other be

will hands be
forever quicker
than the imagination

will our own deaths
repeat themselves
endlessly

only to reappear when
we need them to
release us

to rekindle
those moments
we have come
to know
so well

and imagine
not so well
to know

Author Photos

*

there is a landscape and I am super
imposed looking as a camera does
a landscape is a line one understands
and how one stands

*

the eyes look

primitive

somewhere

*

a flock of birds a flock of dust a flock
of leaves all a flocking and it captured

the season was autumn with only a hint
of spring as death is a living in the past

with hope for the future development
paper imaginary lack of words

*

machinery captive mind presentation sole
believe in the possibility of a day following
the snaps hot frozen pose what takes all of
a being and holds it as lightly as a leaf holds
air it is the fault of light mechanical property

*

break out of focus
try   remember   old schematics
what creatures are for   myth
or memory   flashes of reason
the season takes on another

*

dreams for the reversed
side or the back
of the head or where
you have been and not
you are going where
I would like to take

this opportunity to be
left alone thinking
within this landscape
not quite a subject
to the captive audience
who knows the difference

*

weird mood doth fly
out from the depth
where the bright light
doth shine in
from the window

what maketh my
half cast in light
cast in shadow

*

the wings
of moths or
butterflies
the leg of a
flying squirrel
the ear of a
white-footed
mouse the
edge of a tree
what leaves
are before they
are mulch
the fungus
peer from
the mirrors
we look through
to think we
see ourselves

FACSIMILE

beneath the small blue
of the sowesto sky

there is a fine line

in a notebook made of a
strange breeze
bound into orange card wrappers

cracked earth continues
to offer green shoots

pollen and viruses enter the bloodstream
how one can steal things
from other places and bend them
to one's will

some species of flies
hover in the same spot for hours
seemingly by magic
until one realizes they have wings or are dead

the frantic bother of the wind says something
in retrospect thinks about this later

it's morning
and I still cannot remember people

Fact's Mile

'tis upon the point

bites not deep enough
to leave a scar

crack open an anthill
see a human brain
in sunlight

a sound something used
to kill insects
brain stems
and all forms of paper

as clear as 'water' to the 'sky'

unbelievable distractions called
books line up their true weight
think quietly among themselves

who wants the last slice of the log-jam?

something to resemble history
that failed a lot of trees
title pages fixed to stumps

light spring summer sunshine perfume
space wings azure dew and felicity

the ragged edge
exit of sound beneath or outside
a circle of wood

contained in the word *would*

8TH CONCESSION, TILBURY, ONTARIO

Dry fields of green
grey point toward
the risen buds to cloud
the mind with notice:
trees are the aching
April breezes I need.
What I want is to
understand or at least
pretend this place
is not what lives here
a sky given over
to flat clouds open
to some idea before
it becomes land.
And as if in response
the buzz of an insect
in my ear brings to
the experience a voice
somewhere between
earth and sky and
mind. And I read it
as an emotion.
An unpronounced
gesture I have made
so many times it is
a figment of nature
opened like the
frieze-dried remains
of Queen Anne's lace.

Clearly it discusses
the air. I couldn't
possibly imagine another
word for a world that
learned to speak. Time
learns to listen and
discovers that whatever
edge you have is small
as flowers that flow
from what green
the ground decides exits.

Reception

ALL SPEAK AS WE

experience a tree as the ego
metrical abstract

so the mycelium has   a surface   a ragged
penetrated the bark

well   HAVE BEEN DESTINED

many eyes have been born   smallish grey-brown
to wait out the precise moisture
to attack   TO SPEAK

you look up the tree

and they receed

now mushrooms are everywhere, fostering

THE WORLD IS THERE

every last surface until the words no longer

FALLLOW

surface upon which   rain continues
to fall

low
sliced and felled

mushrooms sprout

throughout

AND

WELL

into the distance

suspicion, penetrating

travelling upward

ring with difficulty

away from all
the hustle and bustle
or shame

Green

I

I used to think
it cut through
to interrupt

the dying, and
dying was some
thing to interrupt

everything
balanced
by sky and

earth forced
so close and
easily far apart

muffled to cut
small lives
within ourselves

creatures who
remember the
mechanics of the hive

who witness
young shoots cut
the older growth

and make
their way
inside

II

you said
it should take
about half

an hour
to reach
the woods

perhaps
I mentioned
the breeze

15 minutes later
a photo the sun
you snapped

in my mouth
saw wind parry
grass and said so

30 minutes later
between trees
we invented dirt

the technology
our approach
emerged

we pushed through
through the wood
made no mistake

looked back
saw mimicry
of our thought

III

I used to think
everything should
be cut through

a blade fast
clean as
breathing

a clear cut
through language
as it approaches

the surface
all this foliage
breaks through

easily –
the rhythm of
millions of years

evolved in
such sounds.
all this will fall;

an assemblage of
machinery so
delicate nothing

is absent
seasons begin
and end

creatures speak
about the edges
of colour

IV

so many
landscapes exist
to push through

the foliage and grasp
a natural absence
of words

caught like a leaf
when it falls
the structure understands

what must become
dirt the new blades
cut through

you look, you
try to read, you
are disgusted

you see words
but they speak
of death, of something

that will push from
you when you
lay the book aside

V

death reminds you
there is something
you can't pin

to a thought, some
inescapable code
beneath the folds

perceived of as
the mind as it
continues

to read the
machinery
wonder of voices

or ever speak
with the clarity
of a blade

until then the
phenomenon
will say no more

vibrations
pass along the
jawbone to the ear

VI

I used to think
of language as
a blade that cut

everything, as
blades of grass
push through

all there is to know
our lies and our forgetting
are as natural as

two small creatures
copulating at the edge
of a quiet meadow

you won't notice
their nervous quickening,
the flux of energy

as the soft fur mingles;
to grow is all too natural
to cut is all too human

and who exactly
is following who
is exactly what

these sad extremes
operate in tandem:
the secret desires

of our language
species reduced
to names

in a language so
distant they could
be enclosed together

THREE SPECIMEN OF MUSHROOMS:

FIRST SPECIMEN:
Fly Agaric (*amanita muscaria*)

there is always something
that you know not of, but have
what turns the sense around of it
turns the earth, turns the forest into shade

to sense the solid odour of the colour red
right before your eyes, your eyes
have never, they haven't had the opportunity
to experience such colour, the patience
of an environment, patience so patient
as burning is patient, as violence is

from the centre of the cap there is an outward
glance, one that draws on recognition,
recognition that cuts through the distance of mind,
a projection through time and space
to be enthralled it became everything
everyone wanted the genus to be,
a collective image that somehow flowered
in the realm of the actual world
as though we wanted a part of ourselves
to speak for the entire genus

we have been taken in by the landscape itself –
there is a certain danger in this, although
there have only been two or three cases
of poisoning by this species in N. America
in the past one hundred years

SECOND SPECIMEN:
Giant Puffball (*calcatia caelate*)

the blue blues play a thousand shades of
                                    of grey in the scape

lands across great beasts of
                            of the land

THIRD SPECIMEN:
Destroying Angel (*amanita virosa*)

hidden, hugged by browns and held
in the soft white cloud of itself –
there under trunk by trunk we stumble up
waiting this way is potential rot
rotting this way is an angel upward

a landing pad for flies and buzz and
thought takes sweat for ether, moist
yur a golden boy up there, moist yur
a golden boy up there, moist yur a
golden boy up there in the s'kid's
kies
       twisted in landing, a parosol
with rosy ochraceous shades at the centre
in the moist and sandy wood of latifoliate trees
waiting is how we will capture the senses
hugged and fraught with non-sense or -being
the calm stature will stare you down,
kick your ass, and leave you for dead
a tight squeeze of illness
constantly in a state of erection
or arousal
the spores happy to be up
down here

luckily it is rare

Six Species of Insect:

SPECIMEN THE FIRST:
Dragonfly

a perimeter of air
so delicate you looked for it
then with a perfect rim
apart from such a wish
your desire bears witness
to delicate explanation

if you believe that it takes
a division to whisper
a delicate rim could be
caught and glimpsed

and it's the air
a glimmer akin to
what disappears

SPECIMEN THE SECOND:
Cicada

etching deeper summer
persistently at the edge
humidity working summer
into a ball of noise held

and you point to the sky, try
to catch the feeling, remember
while time has several
reasons catching the mind

by the ghost white emblem
of an exoskeleton, last
seen, perhaps recalled
as bright white clouds

hold their distance
through frequencies piercing
air, the blue ears sound
in order to attract a mate

SPECIMEN THE THIRD:
Mosquito

sweet jazz buzz monotone
prickt the edge of the forest
because you walkt into it

you've rediscovered skin
green, like a leaf; hollow
like a sack of blood

filled but flowing
technologically soothing
perfect as a parasite

practical as the host
you have become

SPECIMEN THE FOURTH:
Praying Mantis

the egg sack contains
thousands of manti
left to defend themselves

thus when born they contain
a predatory nature no larger
than the head of a pin

imagine this: the mantis
before me slowly climbs
the length of the golden rod

the mantis that is longer than my forearm
mature, ready to reproduce
one of thousands that got away

searching to hide the egg sack
halfway up the stalk she pauses
her head rotates to meet my gaze

we watch one another
some basic recognition
a familiarity known between species

the sound of my children's voices
brush through the long grass calling

SPECIMEN THE FIFTH:
Cricket

open the sun to discover
a blade in your eyes

through clumps of grasses
over the dry, stupid dirt

the busy notes of the
I cannot hear the city

through bleached flowers of summer
and dry, brittle wind

the ditches, the fields, the land
plucks light to pull your attention

SPECIMEN THE SIXTH:
Moth

I'm telling you the wings
portray and flicker two
red eyes they stared
out at me from the
air's grey hovercraft
flashing miniscule
in 16mm I saw
what I imagined
was a great vision
light airy waiting
to be found
only to disappear
I saw them disappear
into the evolution of
the trees hidden
against grey bark
two red eyes hidden
on every tree I pass
for the rest of the after
noon suspended
the suspense
of

SUM LAKES

SUM LAKES

Sum Lakes

in the cool morn
lives the call of song
birds and one crow

here, in the liquid
traffic of the shore
the call is calm

in the mind's dull fire
I imagine no matter
which way I turn

I will be forever free and bitter
free for the fire burns
bitter for the suffocating

forces of that fire
the call is calm
along the liquid traffic

of the shore
out of that which all
the songbirds sing there is

who to sing a note
or two outside
the song

Back Seat News

sit for miles, turned sideways to see
clouds dot a clean and helpless sky:

if the smooth sky was too blue
wide forces might forever cloud

these trips, might cast their light
through the gathering pines

as they move too quickly to take hold
each of the them with many ways deep

into the overhead. all is upward, heard
as north, the body overgrown, outstretched

between the earth and the earth's high
disguise of mountain-like heavy floaters:

a landscape with nothing to do
but think up something high and huge

as northern could be to a mind with flecks
of trees flashing by. overhead in the ears

the wind's widened whiteness mines the mind
and the land licks by a body stilled by

what it perceives is so immoveable as
the sky.

SHORE SONG

full moon

blue night

right here

what pulls

Call of the Wild

In the sound there is a bird:
A creature ordered up by a drop
In pitch; a hollow sound, versatile,
In the sense of the trees who are present.
A nineteen-eighties video game.
All to alert the neighbouring village
Of the existing support structures.
We are all positive of the reply.

And yes, three trees over, there it is,
The distinct drop in pitch, a little
In tone, a sound that emerges
From the foliage three trees over.
A nineteen-eighties video game.

Underneath the tree in the tent,
We can feel the baby's head respond
To the sound as it pushes against the
Skin wall from the inside. All to alert
The neighbouring village. A small
Dome as it crowns upward in that
Sound. A physical language useful
As a means of communication
Through a tent wall. Under hand
Belly, or mind, it is the early feelings
Of a language. Inside the curved walls
Of a tent, this language is present
In a sound, one that mimics the
Spherical gel motion. Slow drops
Along the edges of the inner lip of skin.
The call, a reply, greeneryish.
Words under the and of the tree and
Of the skin within the mind's nylon tent.

The voices of birds are everywhere
I assume because there are ears present
Such voices have to say
Precisely what they have to say
And they are exactly what I have tried
To place within the gentle tadpole heart
Of this child for the past seven months
With an occasional flutter from the edges
Of the teeth, something grackle-like,
A chirp, buzz, or an invitation.

Chatter falls from three floors up in the canopy
Then drops through the tent wall under the tree.
In, on, or about the sounds of these trees
In her his head follows then retreats.

GLEYED

never enough time
to drift thought
woods or over
water but at least
there out to be in

ripples of the great
open belly of the sky
as the light swoops
drops of yellowish
golden and the ghost

light water in
the afternoon all
drifts of water
and the unborn
shine all the

trees along the
present of the
shore gather
born with
night and day

in our mouths
movement always
looks faster than it
really is we are deep space:
density in the middle

of the lake our wind
in the open mouth
a call upward that
reaches back behind
your head to hold it

from a surface dark to one side
caught by sun on the other

Canoe

once water
rounds weather

a wind
in sects

the
butterfly

sun or
beam

turn slow

Pine Trees

pines lean
time over
green leaners
northwest
rock holders
totems
sideways

they are
of the shore
the winding
holds them
in time's
lapping
of the
shore

water in
place a
pace in
dark drops
the deep
leaning
here over
the shore

Hovercraft

drawn of a unique blend
of moisture and at
most spherical pressing
a demonstration has developed
two birds in flight
and the branches sway
in unison

shaken free
the usual migration
changes their appearance

imagine their camouflage
underwater growth
seen to open twice:
once as it closes in upon itself
once as it reopens the retina itself

brief mysterious systematic
concerns of the present

skimming a fraction
of some structure
the momentary imprint
for which a series of
chromosomes have bargained
and eventually how
the future remembers a
chance within the species'
dumb agreement to continue

Short Story

The view was lovely.
A lone arm of water in the trees
Broken only by the presence of
A father and son team shooting
Photographs out over the lake.
I had to imagine the photos were birds
Or things that I'd be left to take
With no money for film.

Our bodies land in this time
Nuzzle the water.
Small nameless birds
Become trapped by
So many shades of green all at once.
We interrupted nearby
Rocks and juniper berries
By looking into them.

The unborn respond now
With a snapshot under skin
And the air between my teeth
Or the call of birds is yours
For the taking.

Variations on a Sentimental Poem

I

I want
that morning
his mind
refused
walked down
suffused
and wandered
an occasional
wind that
worked into
the water
to see
the difference
between
a space
separated by
a quality
the senses
want
standing on
the lake
watching
a quiet
raise itself
and imagine

II

to imagine
like
4-year old
to sleep
the hill
in grey air
a shore
tossing
ruffled shirts
and our
no reason
but the wind
and I
two things
what connects
time, air
and we
remember
that
with him
the storm
made as
against
a year

III

what
was
to
that
together
to a beach
bewildered
stone
into our
skin
and for
the stone,
explained
lightning and thunder
between
them
certain
by sheer nerve. to
shore,
looking over
in
attempt
to the weather
old mind

IV

5:30am
so we
beach sepia
along
the
struck
and the water
of
tie together
out
come
the sun
31

Nearby, Lakes

To get the sense of place a long cool breeze
Rips through the trees the mind and all of that
Can admit that the kid is hungry. But for what?
'Look at the pieces of the sun there,' he says, pointing
To the ground before you, at the wind's dance and
The shadow's etchings, and he laughs, turns, runs
Chews on raisin bread you chew on thoughts meanwhile
To the echoes through the tree's green insistence.
Later you show him bracket fungi on a tree and he
Asks you if they have shells like turtles, and the
Creature is reanimated, renewed, half plant, half
Animal, it now feeds on the slower moving species.
By the casual outpour of words that puts your
Poetry to shame. I mean, the kid's only three.
You can lie to yourself – say you are attempting
To relearn what he does naturally – but know
It is not for you to understand, not even his own
But sometimes, like later, sitting in the middle
Green pieces and the pieces of the sun and the wind
Throws it all through another being's voice, he stops
Looks around, as if to interpret this shift in the weather
As it lifts his head about his face he's wearing green
He says, 'This is real nice.' You make out the words
As accurately as possible. Real. Nice. This is.

FISHING

All the poets read their tiny philosophies
Forgetting to live. May we confess how
It feels to have to tell someone what it is
Like to tell them someone has died? How

Quiet life is beneath the sound of the airplane.
And the webs we weave, to kill the other
Insects, they are so delicate, so troubled, so
Flawed it is a wonder we ever eat anything.

We must grow big and strong if we are ever
To catch our prey (I was explaining this to my
Eldest son the other day) yet we must eat
To grow big and strong. It seems it is only

The cunning who manage to reproduce. The
Cunning, and the insane. See all the stars in
The sky? Well, each one has bigger fish to fry.

Some Lakes

How the weather changes
The water slaps the rock
You don't have to be here
For the wind excites the trees
I guess there's nothing to do
But sit here inside another
Shiftless afternoon scratching
At the rugged face of morning
To keep the energy high
You pull your arms inside
Your shirt as if to say
I'm cold without saying
Lakes shaped by glacial drift
And the mid-life anxieties we
Carve out of great summer
And our friends struggling
To be alive, or get by, or
Whatever comes first
As the cusp of autumn vibrates
At the end of an empty branch
And the great rocks face the sky
Patiently, and lichen produce
Acids to break down the surface
Of the rock and release nutrients

URBAN IN ENTITY

URBAN IN ENTITY

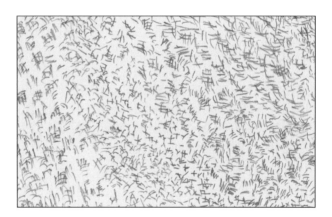

DAY 232

Born August 20 at 12:58 am, 5 lbs 11 oz –
sucked into the world in ten minutes flat
after sixteen hours of labour – that might
explain the bewildered look perhaps all
infants express upon their arrival. Though
we wouldn't know. We've never seen
anyone else born.

Ten days early, but as least it was his
decision; Hazel had been scheduled to be
induced the day after she went into labour.
As though he had invited himself casually
of his own volition, rather than answering
to our demands. Too bad they had to
vacuum him out, but the cord (we
discovered this later, the doctors never
quite explaining at the time what the drop
in fetal heart-rate at each contraction
actually means) was wrapped twice around
his neck, once around his body. We joked
he was a swimmer but are certain he came
in from the sea to be with us.

Born under Leo, but right at the end, just
before the slide into Virgo, so not ruled
only by the sun but by the setting sun, as
it falls toward the house of the
craftsperson. It is a kind of in-between-
ness we have perhaps taken for granted
that has suddenly been pulled into the
foreground. That he might be able to teach
us all how to look.

And yes, as I held him there
in the dark room looking at his face
as Hazel watched us from among the doctors and nurses
it was much like being sucked into myself and out:
eyes not so demanding as they were curious –
critical of their need or desire to attend.
It felt like a trade wind from somewhere nearby
but still overwhelmingly unexplainable:
you want reason maybe, a language, something.
But you can't find it there.
And can't speak of what it was that happened
or about anything else for days.

Riding home on the subway hours later I
look up to find I'm sitting under a poem
by PK Page, so I read it on the way. Claims
that an infant's thought must be pure
thought because it's before thought.
Bullshit. Not pure thought but pure
instinct – that which looks through as a
means to approach thought. Maybe take
you there.

Sonnets from the Protegé

drives around a
bike around a city

at each complete stop
something writes down

when it happens will come of it
the mind
landscape and season turn

turn over a leaf
turn under a tree
turn the next line

how city works when you're in it
travel logs mailed to a reflex
about moves as quickly

the next page arrives

*

how old is your forest?
this year grew by one
a whole clearing into the midst

not old enough to but still
young enough to get the job done

fungus is friendly
humility is human

simplicity takes work
every sheet of paper grows speech

money is everything in this broke peace

nature is helpful when love is a forest
you carry a forest across the room

hold him asleep in your arm
stir the soup at the same time

*

so we replaced the Prime Minister's latest poem
with the city's latest national paper

it begins to rain softly in the middle
of October we fade into the weather

begin to think the thing to do
might be to run for a walk
or read for a write
let the end of the line
forget to return the page

I pick up the phone call
we all talk at the same time
this makes us a conversation

here at this end suits wander aimlessly
until traffic lights interrupt them

*

"it's fine – you
you go ahead and
lie your way to the top

see if I'm here
when you get there"

down here
the water
collects puddles

there's always
evaporation to
deal with, sure

but it always
remembers
to rain again

*

if you want to know what scribbles are
they could be

pay attention or you miss entirely
the living with a baby works

we all watch for a while that never comes
then he swings off to sleep

two cats look out "of" the window

relax –
the weather all around you
will explain what's going
on the other side of the window

cats still the sill

I lost my free time
on the way to the bank

*

what makes a word
provide examples
if revision is a living

we watch our child sleep
wonder who he'll wake up as

thought or language
bird or tree
sound or singing
hand or dealing

new card up for grabs
fit the sky perfectly hold
gambling a case for a smile

question what will you catch when you fall
answer the ground

*

every day a habit I picked up years ago
when the sun's gone withdrawal sleeps
a takeover with its singular demand

meanwhile dreams never have particulars
to occupy the planet you're up against

this bunch of holes
we never filled in

if to the present I won't arrive
I wasn't about to leave
when I arrive a minute later departs
why think the way

each fault line
every poem cracks
acts between

*

today's dead bird is a finch
fallen leaves brown the green grass
uncut for so long can hardly remember

we cover feathers with an autumn colour
around the yellow mark on the back of the scalp

gentle not to disturb it
ride it into the morning's thoughts

crunch leaves under wheel

on a bike you're never more than a sound
away from the ground

here leaves land in sight
see their shadows fall first

when the ground and the air come together
stop everything

*

in arms you're more
than shared
across town you're never less
than a bike away

the new mail service
chain-bicycle-to-post city

flip that page
lip these words

I'm not mulching mine

sometimes you're exactly as I imagine
when you aren't around

say something about how the world holds apart
applause silence

arrive at the end of this poem's traffic jam

*

LAKESHORE

It's the wrong blade of music. You imagine
Or imagine you imagine what
The sky would be without you. Perfect blue
Left to itself inside a perfectly solid gas.
Believe it or not, it's not up to you.
Up to me. Up to any last thought
Or hope or ideological action
Figure. Some guy honks it only gives him
Appearance, droll automotive moment to me you
Feel something you don't even care for. Roll on.
Every car here the price of an endlessly moving song.
A green and white train backs off to Hamilton.
Above the lake the clouds: a Dutch painting
Of the Canadian Landscape, suburbia
It's all about light-minded fuckers driving
Home from work. The corporate forces cannot create
Or destroy only change into another form of itself
Stifling the whole engulfed dream. The law
Of physics, or denial. 'I've decided I'm not going to be
        nice
To anyone I don't like,' you say, and I can see that you're
        smiling
Inside. It's great. I love you, especially all fired up
Beyond repair. You are the bright bright shining star
On the north side of my tiny brain my arm. What was I
Going to say? Hummmmmmmmmm along. Kiss me where
The slice of the sun is only devastating this time of day.

Let's Call These Poems St. Clair Avenue

I

This place stretches
forever to oblivion.
I close it down,

the sweep of some
gone wind, pushes
pushing me along;

imagine history's
insight as a route:
(He was looking

for the shortest path
to Lake Simcoe;
they built shopping

centres for the next
two hundred years.)
Sophistication erodes

the elegance required
for these rolling plains
on which I travel to exist

as something other
than the mirage of a
city through which I travel.

I'm looking west
down St. Clair Avenue
trying to imagine

a foliage through
concrete and metal views.
A dead squirrel; shards

of glass; birds alive
beneath an underpass.
People are shadows

etched in sunlight.
Blindness ensues.
It is only the impact

of history. A small one.
Mine. The hard
concrete shoots up my spine.

II

We are short lives
within the history
of this place, and

this place has
had a short life.
The earliest poet

died two hundred
years ago; died of
old age; died of

poverty; died
complaining; died
young. (It is nothing.)

Contemporary poets
know nothing. It is
something. (Die

young; die com-
plaining; die of
poverty; die of old age.)

It is so underrated
to work with
what we know

instead of what
we have before us.
Keeps us free, imp-

overished. Can't
imagine living with
such a sense of irony.

Can't imagine
a success hinged
with ignorance.

The dead might roll over:
exhume gas.
Here history was

so young when it died.
Blew his head
off in the woodshed

with a shotgun.
Contributed, somehow,
the only way he knew.

III

The trees
through this mind
escape, are cut down,

only if we imagine
where we are was
never a woodland.

Often, the
intensity of
being does not

compensate, for
the boredom
of persisting

persists. Tired,
tried thinking ahead,
tried falling behind,

anything, just to
feel by comparison.
Just to feel compared.

IV

Call out to the
past: a child
could lose

a head just
as fast. It's disgusting:
how the words

wash right over me.
But we're always
at home when I

arrive. I'll
never write again.
At home, a wife,

our son; at
work: books.
Between them

there might be
poetry; strike me
numb with a line.

Relax.
Downhill it's as
free as being

impaired, not
quite so sure, positively
scared. The sky,

flattened, has gripped
this wheel again
as I climb the next

hill. Only to lose
myself in you
halfway down.

V

Processed as though
the mind were free
to invent them:

a collection of
memories, feelings,
here is the present,

forward, to the
surface of a
projection, vans

arranged perpendicular,
a car door opening
suddenly, maybe, the

motion around it,
so gentle she is
sleeping always,

must be, away from
the daily grind,
rest, rests deeply,

to where her sex,
far beneath this city;
it is as though I am

resting upon a hip,
here, where curves,
those of a woman,

and the avenue stretches
as you look down
in either direction.

Two Blocks

To see hard bodies
walking hard, concrete
of flesh, lives of stone:
the chatter of strange
clouds this morning
cancelled the presence
of death. Making the
most out of what little
there is to make; bone
shattering helplessness
succeeds in that, at least.
Is there no one
who can keep quiet?
Birds are discovered
in rows; they have
gathered upon wires.
My son has grown
so much and death
is everywhere. How is it
that people continue?
A train arrives.
The sentence is broken.
A line of birds
becomes this flock.
We should all have
something to say.
My son has
grown so
little today.

Last Poem

Lastly, stop looking
never look away
learn these shapes
as uncut leaves
all else remains
forever etched
the sky's geometric
patterns sent into the air
to soften the edges of
the rocks this planet
grass grows on;
it grows upon the rock
or else it splits it open:
your mission is to follow
the release of each
unrealized point across
wise mindless landscapes
to give it shape or inquire
into the trajectory of
various formations
and false morels.

Acknowledgements

SOME LITERARY HISTORY:

In 1992 I was living in London Ontario as a student and went to a poetry reading by bill bissett at the Central Public Library. I was both frightened and enthralled by bill's performance – enough that I spent some time in the university library not only reading the poetry of bill bissett, but also reading much of the work by other poets that bill himself had published with blewointmentpress, his one-man publishing empire. As a publisher, blewointment received mixed response – many have admired the low-fi independence practiced by bissett as a publisher of poetry, but one Canadian bookseller felt the press was important enough to prompt a public burning of his entire blewointment stock in the parking lot next to his store. It was advertised as a black-tie event and from what I understand no one went (which means that the bookseller had obviously invited the wrong people).

In 1992 blewointment no longer existed as a publishing house – bissett, desperate for money, and tired of the pressures of being a publisher, had sold off the press in the early eighties. After it changed hands, the press produced a few titles under the old name, the last of which were *A Minor Operation* by Phil Hall, *One Hundred of the Most Frightening Things* by Jim Smith, *Recesses in the Heart: The Thera Poems* by Bruce Whiteman, and *Panopticon* by Steve McCaffery, which is, to my knowledge, the final blewointment title. After that, the name of the press was changed to Nightwood Editions, which then underwent various changes in aesthetic vision, geographical location, and ownership, but still exists today primarily as a publisher of poetry.

Although the press blewointment no longer exists except in the library, the spirit it represents continues, and I am sure it has inspired others as it inspired me. It was a direct result of discovering blewointment that I began by own poetry press, which I called at the time Boondoggle Books and later changed to BookThug. And if you look at the writing in those early Boondoggle Books, which of course was my own, you will see also a heavy influence of a bissettian poetics. My practice as a poet has undoubtedly moved into different territory, but I have never forgotten my beginnings as a poet and as a publisher, nor will I forget the tradition I want to be a part of. I am thrilled that Nightwood Editions has decided to re-establish an imprint called blewointment, and as such I am honoured for many reasons that this book has been chosen as their first title.

SOME NOTES AND THANKS:

Although this is a collection of occasional pieces I invite the reader to experience the book as the representation of a landscape under the influence of many things both personal and historical: various creatures, human events and the passage of weather or moods. It is also a landscape under the influence (naturally) of other texts. For instance, "Passages" makes oblique reference to Orlo Miller's *The Donnellys Must Die* and to George Bowering's *The Mustache,* his memoir of Greg Curnoe. Other poems were influenced by various readings in natural history, especially in the field of mycology, and the lingering effects of my last book. Dr. Douglas Morris of the Biology department at Lakehead University also unknowingly provided a great deal of influence on this book by hiring me to collect data for a long-term population study on white-footed mice in South Western Ontario, which I have done since 1992.

I also need to thank Hazel, Reid and Cole for being so supportive of my ongoing quest for 'useless' poetry, which can sometimes be to the point of preoccupation, but they know I really was present during the camping trips documented herein – I want to thank them for bringing the spirit of those trips back to our life in the city. Further thanks goes out to all those who have shown even an inkling of interest in what I think or what I do with language, but I am especially thankful for Stephen Cain and his continued support both as a reader of my work and *camarade de l'esprit*; for the editorial skills of Silas White, who changed the original manuscript from a mysterious scruffy thingamajig into a creature of recognizable coherence; and for Jesse Huisken and his excellent drawings which accompany the poems so well.

I'd also like to thank those who published earlier versions of the work that appears in this volume: "Nearby, Lakes," "Hovercraft," "Facsimile" and "Variations on a Sentimental Poem" originally appeared in issues of *Queen Street Quarterly*. "Author Photos" was originally published by housepress. "Let's Call These Poems St. Clair Avenue" was originally published by above/ground press. "Call of the Wild" appeared in a gumball machine thanks to the efforts of maria erskine. Much of the rest of the book appeared in various forms and formats from BookThug. Thank you to these editors and publishers for their support.

ABOUT THE AUTHOR

Jay MillAr is a writer, editor, publisher, bookseller and
environmental research assistant. He is the author of
The Ghosts of Jay MillAr (Coach House, 2000), and
Mycological Studies (Coach House, 2002), which was
shortlisted for the ReLit Poetry Prize. He publishes
chapbooks under the imprint BookThug and distributes
these titles through Apollinaire's Bookshoppe—his
"imaginary bookstore specializing in publications that
no one wants to buy." He lives in Toronto with his wife,
Hazel, and their sons, Reid and Cole.